A FEW WOR|

Adam Crittenden ⟨...⟩ during times of impending doom (mythological, Biblical, psychological, imaginal). Give this book a chance to show you its necessities, to demonstrate what ink and paper can continue to do that flesh and blood cannot. In a century where a face can be successfully transplanted, why not a voice? Who doesn't want to be remade? Go ahead. Traipse into this twisted forest (before the first light bulb falls), and you might well agree that "we should have left / after the first few minutes / but by now it is too late."

~Timothy Liu
author of *Don't Go Back to Sleep*

In BLOOD EAGLE, Adam Crittenden's moving and complex collection, the narrator cries, "What I wouldn't give for a little death," which in the world of Crittenden's fascinating poems means: what I wouldn't give to feel, what I wouldn't give to understand, what I wouldn't give to be human, for how can we be human when "all we've ever done is pretend." These poems read as if written "on the glass with bloody fingernails." They are painful, sometimes frightening, and always interesting.

~Peter Grandbois
author of *Nahoonkara*

If illness is a motif of Adam Crittenden's provocative debut collection, BLOOD EAGLE, it affects not only the body but the body politic, and poems about the degeneration of the individual converse with poems about the devolution of culture. It would be a dreary forecast indeed if not for the intimate voice that consoles as it dissects, reminding us that all is not lost and that "happiness" is still possible if, like surgeons, we "look at the parts and not the whole." For Crittenden, language is a lancet, and with it he cuts to save himself and us.

~Daniel Mueller
author of *Nights I Dreamed of Hubert Humphrey*

"I had not thought death had undone so many," Dante said upon entering the underworld; six centuries later, Eliot quoted him in The Waste Land. In BLOOD EAGLE, Adam Crittenden traces the reverberation of such awe through the underworld of our own time, where bodies are vivisected, beset by parasites, and torn asunder by personal apocalypse. At times both surreal and mundane, Crittenden's dark lyrics navigate through strip clubs and apartment caves, dance parties and Disneyland, witnessing the detritus of late empire, a culture ready "for divination, but not ready / for the divination to be true." In this powerful, often unsettling book, Crittenden seeks the truth through unflinching engagement with word, world, and mind. With Blood Eagle, he becomes our guide in a quest for what is really real.

~Joshua McKinney
author of *Mad Cursive*

Einarr made them carve an eagle on his back with a sword, and cut the ribs all from the backbone, and draw the lungs there out, and gave him to Odin for the victory he had won.

~*The Orkneyinga Saga*, circa 1230

Gold Wake presents

ADAM CRITTENDEN's

BLOOD

EACLE

Copyright © 2016 by Adam Crittenden

Published by Gold Wake Press

Cover design by Nick Courtright
nickcourtright.com

Cover images from *Gray's Anatomy* by Henry Gray,
"Torn Paper" by Elnur, and the author

No part of this book may be reproduced
except in brief quotations and in reviews
without permission from the publisher.

10 9 8 7 6 5 4 3 2 1

Blood Eagle
2016, Adam Crittenden
adamcrittenden.com

goldwake.com

TABLE OF CONTENTS

[To Us]

THE ENDING IS FOREVER THE SAME
AND THAT IS THAT IT ENDS

My eyes twitch

       and these lungs

spread backward.

       No, they do backflips

until sleep comes.

       I am stuffed into

this body we call a body and these

feathers we call our feather and these cells

our cell.

This is our tumor, and our brains

       play with our brains

and this play repeats.

There is a self-destruction button lodged

in my windpipe. You come up to me

               and smell me, and you say

I am rotting from the inside out,

and I say fuck you, but in short you are right.

        When we argue we argue

like no others—we embrace each failed cell

and face off like barbarians ready to paint the sky

        with sloppy swords.

[Let's take a moment to remember who we are. I am the
beloved. You are the beloved. You are the hero. I am the
anti-hero. You are the anti-hero. I am the anti-hero. You are
Penelope. I am Odysseus. You are Odysseus. I am
Penelope. You are blood. I am marrow. You are marrow. I
am oxygen. You are not hate. I am not love. We will not
remember any of this by the end.]

This violence is not your violence,

nor mine, but ours.

In this realization

the moon melts into the sun

and the tide freezes

because it has nothing else to do.

TRIAGE

I throw a fistful of leeches

        at the wound, and this is when

you remind me that we're beyond leeches.

Specifically, we are at the point

        where we need to get our priorities right.

When we stroll through our empty house

        we realize that all we've ever done

is pretend to be human. We've cut the superfluous limbs

        and cauterized them to limit the bleeding.

We've repeated the behaviors

        of our neighbors, our celebrities,

                those we call our friends—

                    our family.

        You tell me I've lost the ability to copy

        and paste

the husks of others onto my person.

I've never been more scared in my

life—

actually, I've never been scared

until now.

YOU MAINTAIN EVERYTHING
IS FANTASY PART I

~Remake of "Poem" by Auden

You maintain everything is fantasy

ringing in our ears

because it makes you feel safe

like your mom's womb—tucked away

in a sweet placenta

pit of happiness.

We used to take walks in nearby meadows

to see all their flowers and bees,

but now concrete and circuits

seem more our style.

I watch football on our flat-screen.

Then I don't watch football

on our flat-screen because let's be honest—

I don't care. This is an illusion to say I am here

and I have a cock.

YOU MAINTAIN EVERYTHING
IS FANTASY PART II

~Remake of "Poem" by Auden

My grandfather's ghost walks in

and tells me a joke:

"Your grandfather's ghost walks in

and tells you a joke."

He [it] doesn't worry about irony.

He [it] says we fizzle

in an acidic tomb, asleep and stone-like

and placid.

The football ends. We flip the channels

and the newest version of *Spider-man*

airs on HBO. You tell me you are ready

for the next version—see what they will do next.

I DON'T HAVE A BEAK,
BUT WILL THIS DO?

I am not prepared

      to have this conversation right now.

      But we are having it—

we are having it right now.

      You ask me if I want

to be alone. Then you don't want

me to answer that question.

[The world is brutal, yes, but if you look closely there is still
happiness. It reveals itself like a stain on dark jeans. You see
it and then you don't. This is how happiness works and
there are few exceptions, if any.]

Coral crystalizes outside our window,

and this is no surprise. I didn't count on changing

as much as I did, or becoming

an atrophied shell, swallowed by salty murk.

Yes, my love, we are going

to a dark place.

YOU'RE IMMORTAL,
BUT YOU DON'T KNOW IT YET

You hang me

on the mounted branched antlers

pushing my lungs through

my chest for me

to look down on—

such an unfamiliar part

of this body.

There is no blood; instead,

there is water. The water runs

to your feet and you shiver

because it's cold.

You tell me your children love you

and maybe they do,

but maybe they don't.

You will find out when they try to kill you.

HOW TO LIVE FOREVER

["Walt Disney was born in Chicago, IL on December 5, 1901. In 1906, his family moved to a Missouri farm, where he had an idyllic early childhood and first learned to draw. The farm failed, and in 1911 his family moved to Kansas City, MO where he rose at 3:30 a.m. to deliver newspapers on his father's paper route and fell in love with vaudeville and movies. In 1917, the family moved to Chicago, where Walt created cartoons for his high school yearbook, took classes at the Art Institute of Chicago, and tried to enlist in the U.S. Army. Rejected for being underage, he joined the American Ambulance Corps and arrived in France as World War I ended. When Walt returned to the United States, he settled in Kansas City and got a job at a commercial art studio. In 1920, while working at an ad company, Walt discovered the fantastical world of animation and immersed himself in the young medium. While keeping his day job, he began making Laugh-O-gram ad reels and animation shorts with artist Ub Iwerks. Laugh-O-grams Films soon went bankrupt, and Walt, at age 21 moved to California with $40 in his pocket."

http://www.waltdisney.org/beginnings-walt-disney%E2%80%99s-early-years-1901-1923]

I told you to not believe
that Walt Disney's
disembodied head
is cryogenically
frozen somewhere
below the Matterhorn

[disembodied
adjective
1. separated from or existing without the body: *a disembodied ghost*
2. (of a sound) lacking any obvious physical source: *a disembodied voice at the end of the phone*

http://oxforddictionaries.com/definition/disembodied?reg

ion=us&q=disembodied]

because there is one

absolute truth in this world:

you can only be a piece

of paper and some ink

in the end.

You sipped your coffee

and said, *"I bet Disney is still alive,*

and his new body is a robot spider."

HOT SLUG

Earlier that morning,

you knew

      the implications of war,

           and what's more,

      you knew

there is always war.

      When the bullet hits

it cools, and in doing so

the slither

           through flesh ceases.

I can't speak

      for you, but

I can load your wounds

with earth.

As it rains, I walk

in the park to kill time.

      The drops drench

me thoroughly

            while people hustle

            back into their homes

like ticks into skin.

CARTILAGE

      I cut myself

into segments for accounting purposes.

[We will all be objectified. We will all be seen as parts and
not people. We can still find happiness in such a world if
we look at the parts and not the whole.]

Yes, I still have a stomach

      and a heart and a brain.

My lungs carry a chunk of my torso away—

it flies north for the winter—

      and I don't miss that piece.

[*What Can Be Donated*

"The organs of the body that can be transplanted at the
current time are kidneys, heart, lungs, liver, pancreas, and

the intestines. Kidney/pancreas transplants, heart/lung transplants, and other combined organ transplants also are performed. Organs cannot be stored and must be used within hours of removing them from the donor's body. Most donated organs are from people who have died, but a living individual can donate a kidney, part of the pancreas, part of a lung, part of the liver, or part of the intestine."

http://www.organdonor.gov/about/donated.html]

You see the partial me

      when you get home from work.

      You don't notice the change

            and I'm being flexible—I don't care.

FLOWERED ELYSIUM

Leaves break down

      under the stress of children

who walk to school

         along streets littered

with grass-clippings and plastic bags

of waste.

Cold pastoral

fell like empires and termite hills.

      Empire rose, again.

Some hug the rapture.

        Wheat browns and yields

    its clusters,

bent, spent after

another season.

Sometimes I take old possessions,

like the clay cups I made in elementary school,

and shatter them.

I like purging things:

purging my house and my car

of trash, purging my guilt

or my responsibilities

with the hope that one day I will be

reduced

to the minimum amount of me.

The mist of a brook turns

into a smack of water,

salmon and pebbles—

what I wouldn't give

for a little death.

I can't leave.

I can't leave because

the vines grasp,

      pull, and withhold

      until the I is no longer.

ODYSSEUS
AND THE STRIPPING SIRENS

Without hesitation,

    the sirens of the cave slapped their curves

on the laps of the lotus eaters.

They slid up

    and down

    the screeching

poles

    and the lotus eaters ate

with dilated pupils.

    Destiny and Serenity floated onto

    Odysseus' worn lap,

and they promised

him the lotus of a lifetime.

Destiny's black cobalt cross
bounced between her tits,
and Odysseus found himself
gazing at the hypnotic necklace.

Even as it rippled,
the silicone held elegance,
exposing the slightest of scars.

Serenity sung.
Odysseus rose.
His crew was dead.
They represented all
he neglected in the world.
He reached into his pocket for money
but found a handful of tapeworms.

POSSESSED, BUT THE OPPOSITE

~Remake of "Poem" by Bishop

Nobody gets paintings of themselves

done anymore,

but if you knew a guy

you would.

I believe this because of the way you squint

your eyes when you smile—you don't

want anyone to see your crazy eye teetering

off into a psychotic distance.

The car radio plays a remix

of Nirvana and techno:

[*Here we are now, entertain us.*

I feel stupid and contagious.]

We drive across the earth's crust

in search of your family. They have dispersed

and fled into the collateral people,

escaping their memories of you

because they think there's a devil

growing within your meat,

waiting to burst open and shed you

like a wet coat.

They don't know that instead

you shed the little devil—a relic of imagination

that didn't have a snowball's chance

because you were much, much worse than it was.

EMPIRE MIND

growth

is not always pleasing

it's a cold day

            in the halls of overgrown columns
 the realm transfigures us

                and we become trash
the ancient heroes and villains and in-betweens
remain today in one form or a hundred

       the empire's destruction is happiness

we embrace the shadow of the individual life
     a green mist

I want skeletons to rise

weeds grow in animal motion

       only to shrink and shrivel

as if

       seasons elapse in seconds

     teenagers spin the bottle on a flat tombstone

       they press faces

       burrow into the ground

it's a blank

       above the lit city

         every photon

eats our knowledge

and we didn't want this kingdom after all

we trace a shadow for life

it's a hot day

       on the tracks of a train

the realm makes metal

          a shackle

we don't mind being bound

as long as it's on our terms

I'm only a curator

in this realm

        I have nothing else

except a few bent skyscrapers

            collapsed because they can

let's move on

because we can

let's eat yellow jewels

to ease our rusted stomachs

        would you rather

            fall asleep on a thousand shards

of broken beer bottle glass

or have your eardrums

      vacuumed out

and no

you don't have another choice

in the matter

again

you don't have another choice

in the matter

      again

      you don't have another choice in the matter

here's what we know for sure

warning

usually when we hear that

we get bullshit

we think therefore we are

      an empire is only as strong as its rival empires

we don't have another choice in the matter

      it's too easy to say empires rise and fall

it's too singular to say we are empire

how dare we claim such status

do we have choices in the matter

are we part of said we

we don't have another choice in the matter

again

we don't have another choice in the matter

would you rather

cannibalize your head

or cannibalize someone else's

I'LL SHOW YOU MY GOD
IF YOU SHOW ME YOURS

I killed myself with pills.

    A lot of pills. I think

    they were Oxycodone,

but I'm not sure.

I woke up in a desert of apples.

    It's simple, really,

        the sand wasn't sand,

but it was apples.

I began biting

into one apple, then another,

and another, and I looked down

    at my stomach,

    and it was a large apple.

It burst open

    with my last bite,

and the pills spewed

to the apple ground.

I tried as hard as I could

        to understand why apples

    of all things, but nothing

came to me, so I closed

my eyes and prayed

for answers, for closure.

        I didn't know

which god was listening,

    so I prayed to them all.

WE USED TO PLAY SUPER NINTENDO FOR FUN

~Remake of "Poem" by Creeley

If water

takes the form of weeds,

and the weeds

the form of stones,

then it's simple:

a short life is a happy one.

I go to an underground fashion party

where my friends

throw dusty clumps of coke

into the flashing air and bathe

in the dry rain.

[This isn't real after all. This isn't real, after all. After all, this isn't real. This, after all, isn't real. All isn't real after this. After real this isn't all.]

We agree that we should have left
after the first few minutes
but by now it is too late.

Our skin is transparent
and our veins are white—bloating
and dry-heaving from being packed
with powder blood. A reckoning
of sorts seems overdue.

DANCE PARTY

If the strobe lights stay on

                    too long,

then the cadaver faces

          of all the dancers appear.

Their faces will frown

and we'll love ourselves

                a little more,

                only because their lives

are worse than ours.

I am a human piece

of glitter, my throat

          ripped open for entertainment

but I get revenge

when I steal their veins,

place them in jars,

and stir the contents.

This shiny city was something

                 when our world began,

                 but now it's cracked;

even the flamingos sulk,

screeching because it has clipped their wings.

FINGERING THE SKY

The snow outside

the skyscraper's window

        drops slowly,

and so much sorrow

      explodes

      into the red air.

      You gesture for me

      to come closer

with your clumsy index finger

and hazy smile,

but this is just to say

that you want me

      to ignore my self-hatred

        and insecurities.

The night's poison of choice

slips and slides in our bloodstreams,

      punishing our livers until

      we acquiesce like trained mice.

When you point you don't point

      at me, but at the space

      you can't occupy, a distance measured

      by all the cells in your body connected

like a fragile string or fleshy cobweb.

THE ILLUSION

~Remake of "Poem" by Notley

Through the screens

of my apartment cave

the midnight greens

fluctuate in a sky

of chemicals and dead breath

from dead people

sunken in a dead city,

like an Atlantis that isn't lost

or underwater or Atlantis.

From this perch of mine

you can see St. Mark's Place

trapped in a heap of cobwebs

that aren't really cobwebs,

but Halloween decorations.

You can also see

Tompkins Square Park

vibrating like a bass drum

and shaking the nearby bricks

to dust. I've coined this process

as the Tompkins Process.

I don't know who Tompkins is

or was, but now her [or his] namesake

is only a process for me to process.

It's not surprising that the night's air

is hot and boils skin

or that the green hues

permeate our surfaces,

but it is surprising

that we were the illusion.

OUR MODERN DILEMMA

Sterile doctors don't know

           what to do with us,

so they eat our yellowing bodies

to the bone.

[Remember when I said there is happiness in the world—

you just have to know where to look? It's not here.]

           We grow back,

regenerating in frightening fits.

I am in one room, isolated,

           as are you,

       but we can see each other

through the glass. I notice a handprint smudge

       from the previous patient.

46

They take you from your room

       and that's the last of you.

       The new patient writes a message

on the glass with his bloody fingertips;

I can't read it but I know it's important—

       this is how signs work.

THE NEIGHBOR SCREAMS. WHY?

You and I

    peak through the window,

    hoping that everything is alright

        but we're secretly excited at the same time.

From window to window

    we see that their living room

        is filled with blue water—a fish tank

        littered with a weightless sectional couch,

    a black coffee table,

    among other loose furniture.

    The neighbors float by as well.

Funny, we never even talked to them.

"I HAVE A BAD FEELING ABOUT THIS"

~Remake of "Poem" by Simic

Every morning I forget

how it is

that my shoes appear

at the foot of my bed.

Earlier this morning,

I reached for one

and happened to notice

a wormhole inside.

The foot-sized portal

revealed a labyrinth

of magma and minerals,

quartz and skeletons.

Is this hell?

[I wondered.]

I walked to the corner store

in my wormhole shoes, fearing

that I might slip

and fall into the earth's core—

a second later I fell into the earth's core.

There was happiness there,

believe it or not.

The carcasses of people

from the past sat

beautifully in their respective thrones

of crystals and stalactites

and stalagmites.

I woke up in my bed.

If my shoes could talk,

they would ask how I got there.

I REMEMBER WHEN WE SAW
THE FUTURE IN A GOAT'S ENTRAILS

I was the hero back then

    but time changes ethics.

    It faded the importance of things

        like the sun bleaches algae

and turns it fossil white.

    The world was ready

        for divination, but not ready

        for the divination to be true.

    Red and purple fireworks bleed

down on us while we kiss at the river's edge.

    This moment is fated, meaning

        that I couldn't have stopped it

        even if I tried.

Two owls stalk mice

     and shred the tiny meat—

not for predictions or superstitions

     or politics or religion or science

     or money or fame

or greed or want or sex

       or entertainment or respect

       or knowledge,

     but because that's what owls do.

THE DUCK POND

I snatch pieces of you

and chuck them

at the dark green pond.

It only takes one

duck to detach

from the pack

and notice you bobbing around

here and there

to start dinner.

Half of your face

is all that's left

and your one empathetic eye

blinks puppy-esque,

making the argument that I should spare

your final pieces.

But those goddamned ducks

are so very hungry,

ruffled and insane

and soft and happy.

MEMORIAL FOR WHAT
COULD HAVE BEEN

~Remake of "Poem" by Paz

Because you're a visual creature.

That's why.

That's why you sat in the park

and compared people to movie characters.

There's James Bond. Not Connery. The creepy one from the

eighties.

You wonder where your favorite fictional people are at this

moment.

[Maybe Bruce Wayne is eating roasted lamb with Clarice

Starling. When she smiles, he smiles. He wants to say he's a

sociopath and that it's alright because he's a good one.

Clarice scrapes her fork on the expensive dish and Bruce

grits his teeth—not for the sake of the dish but for the sake of his well-being. The metal against porcelain reminds him of his deceased parents. The sound triggers a memory so faint it's like vapor. He remembers being scolded for playing with his food, and he wants to be scolded again.]

When you leave the park

you notice a sunburnt cross

on the side of the interstate. It marks a quaint cliff

and as you drive you feel vertigo,

but it's not—it's what you think

vertigo should feel like.

WHEN THE BODY COMMITS SUICIDE

Maybe the cells will have a change of heart.

Maybe they won't replicate at a rate

        so ridiculous that the biological

    game of chicken reaches the cliff.

        This is the part where organs explode

into masses of self-destruction.

I always wondered if spontaneous combustion was real and

yes,

it is, but it doesn't end in fire.

      When I first found out my body was killing itself

        I sprawled prone on the bed,

           downing water

        and aloe juice,

         praying with as much conviction

as possible, trying to understand

　　　why my cells didn't want to live

anymore,

　　　just like everyone else's.

YES. RIGHT NOW WOULD BE
A GREAT TIME FOR YOU TO TELL ME
THAT I AM NOT BEING EATEN
BY A GIANT GUT WORM

We sit on the city balcony

        above the ant people and drink margaritas

                with amaretto shots.

I have my doubts

—this is nothing new—

            and you say

there is nothing to worry about. Everything is going to be

fine.

        You reach for my stomach and insert

your open hand through my belly button.

                    I feel your hand fish

around,

tickling my innards until you say

there is nothing to worry about. Everything is

going to be fine.

I am depressed right now.

And you remind me that everyone else is, too.

You say everyone is depressed

and everyone is a sociopath,

but some people hide things

better than others.

THE WAX MUSEUM

~Remake of "Poem" by Williams

There are endless reasons

why we failed as people. Maybe

it began when I received a card

from you and never wrote back.

I thought I would have written back,

but, you know.

I remember the Alamo

reenactors and how we wondered

if being one was a full-time job.

You pointed at Davy Crockett

and said, *"what about him?"*

"He's a part-time plumber

who divorced recently. He comes out

here on Tuesdays and Thursdays

because he enjoys the history.

After the second month

[*of reenacting*], *he began to hate*

the tourists—especially the tourists

who confused him with Daniel Boone.

Once he's upset, he gets more upset

with himself because he didn't do well

in high school history, and he wishes he had

because he liked his teacher."

You said I could not be

further from reality. You said,

"he's happily married

and moonlights as a chef,

but he doesn't need to because his family's

incredibly wealthy—God wealthy."

We crossed the street and entered

the wax museum. There was a massive Predator

[replica] that I had to take a picture with

and I didn't know whether to smile or not.

THE BOY WHO HAD A SEA-SNAIL
GROWING IN HIS KNEE

Maybe fifteen years from now

    the boy will remember

  what it was like

to have a pet

    growing

inside of himself,

  depending on its host

to be kind. Or maybe

    he won't.

  Eventually,

    the internet forgets

    his story

     and the snail is long dead,

     its cells

and molecules spread

across the city

like microscopic tableaus

for a scavenger hunt

nobody cares about.

In fact, I see the boy now

riding the subway to his cubicle.

I LICK YOUR PUPILS

They taste sour like lemons—

    only at first, though.

      In seconds

    chemicals swish in my skull

    until I can't take it anymore

and collapse in your family room.

I never noticed how your ceiling fan is modern.

My eyes vibrate until the taste of you

    translates into seeing what you have seen,

    experiencing what you have experienced.

    You hate people.

I had no idea.

You always seem so friendly and cheery.

When I awake from the hallucinatory teardrop trip,

I see you hovering over my body with a blue glass of water

asking if I'm alright,

your look of concern concealing

the fact that you are

mad at the world

and even more mad at yourself.

MARRIED PEOPLE

~Remake of "Poem" by O'Hara

["Lana Turner had an acting ability that belied the 'Sweater Girl' image MGM thrust upon her, and even many of her directors admitted that they knew she was capable of greatness (check out *The Postman Always Rings Twice* (1946)). Unfortunately, her private life - seven marriages, affairs almost too numerous to mention, a long bout with alcoholism and the famous incident where her gangster lover, Johnny Stompanato, was killed by her daughter, Cheryl Crane - came to overshadow her professional accomplishments."

http://www.imdb.com/name/nm0001805/bio?ref_=nm_o v_bio_sm]

We watch *Imitation of Life*

while sharing a bowl of vanilla bean

ice cream. The rain splattering on the roof

mutates into hail and I worry about our car.

Meanwhile, the bookshelf collapses

and splinters to the floor,

dropping a cascade of books and particle board.

We go to bed, leaving the broken shelf

and pile for tomorrow

or maybe for the next weekend.

As it turns out, we never fix the shelf

and we shove the books in a box

in the garage. We tell ourselves

we'll invest in a new shelf soon.

SHE HAS A BULLET
WITH MY NAME ON IT

I discovered her in the attic,

        shrunken and mad, her arms

        folded like a spiteful wall

    of flesh wrapped

    in a black and white blouse.

    Her dad's gold pocket-watch hung

        from the wall stud, gigantic

and bold and haunting.

The gun poking out behind her

        didn't bother me as much

as the pink and white cake

        resting in the middle of the room.

        She was a Miss Havisham reborn,

        a hell-bent figure that was no longer

my lover but an antagonist.

[Let's take a moment to remember who we are. I am the beloved. You are the beloved. You are the hero. I am the anti-hero. You are the anti-hero. I am the anti-hero. You are Penelope. I am Odysseus. You are Odysseus. I am Penelope. You are blood. I am marrow. You are marrow. I am oxygen. You are not hate. I am not love. We will not remember any of this by the end.]

I thought of leaving the room,

but the door seemed small

and impossible to find.

THE HAPPIEST PLACE ON EARTH

~Remake of "Poem" by Notley

Our animatronic summers

at Disneyland made us forget

the wars we committed to—the wars

we shook on and agreed to.

Later that year [in the winter]

cows surrounded us,

their backs glazed in snow

and their hooves dipped

in flat brown patties.

More time elapses.

I cock my head to the right

because it makes my neck feel better,

or perhaps the world's poles

are up to something again.

You ask me if I have dreamed lately

and I quickly say no

because it's true and I've noticed it as well.

WE JUST AREN'T RIGHT
FOR EACH OTHER ANYMORE

She believed

it was about to rain

light bulbs. The first bulb

fell from the clouds, exploding

on the forest floor.

She expected more

to come as the bitter halogen

smell hit her nose,

but the storm never came.

She ate the filament

and said it tasted like the opposite

of what she once believed we were.

THEODOR ADORNO'S
ZOMBIE CORPSE

~Remake of "Poem" by Notley

It was the afternoon of November

15th last fall and Theodor [Ted]

Adorno's zombie corpse

rose from its German gravesite

and toured the world speaking

of globalization and the degeneration of art.

["Unlike today's malevolent movie zombies, the original

Haitian zombies were not villains but victims. They are

corpses who have been re-animated and controlled by

magical means for some specific purpose (usually labor).

Historically, fear of zombies was used as a method of

political and social control in Haiti. Those people believed

to have the magical power to zombify a person -- mainly

75

witch doctors called *bokors* -- were widely feared and respected. *Bokors* were also believed to be in service of the Tonton Macoute, the brutal and much-feared secret police used by the oppressive Duvalier political regimes (1957-1984). Those who defied authorities were threatened with becoming the living dead—a concern not taken lightly."

http://news.discovery.com/history/history-zombies-12-6-4.html]

When he [it] came to Manhattan
several rats scampered
from the sewers and ate him [it],
and he [it] was dead again—the leftovers
illuminated by the seascape's twilight.

["Conflict and consolidation marked the last decade of Adorno's life. A leading figure in the "positivism dispute" in German sociology, Adorno was a key player in debates about restructuring German universities and a lightning rod for both student activists and their right-wing critics. These controversies did not prevent him from publishing numerous volumes of music criticism, two more volumes of *Notes to Literature*, books on Hegel and on existential philosophy, and collected essays in sociology and in aesthetics. *Negative Dialectics*, Adorno's magnum opus on epistemology and metaphysics, appeared in 1966. *Aesthetic Theory*, the other magnum opus on which he had worked throughout the 1960s, appeared posthumously in 1970. He died of a heart attack on August 6, 1969, one month shy of his sixty-sixth birthday."

http://plato.stanford.edu/entries/adorno/]

He [it] spawned new artists,

but those artists spawned

new forms of cooptation

and more reality shows.

I saw the whole thing happen

through a lowered tear beyond

the apartment cave window

and there were azure gods—

their presence dewy and heavy.

REMNANTS

The hot desert bloomed

with bleached carcasses and trash

and the heat fenced us in—

all that was left for us to do in our

apocalypse

was to smoke and drink

until our breakfasts flopped

from our mouths and splashed to the dry

soil.

The earth consumed

our cells

and matter, but the amalgamation

of earth and man was not natural.

It was like planting a plastic

bottle

in the ground, then waiting

for a bottle tree to grow.

One of the smokers and

drinkers

told me that the whole planet will be dust soon.

He sucked in, spewed

a cloud,

and dug his boots

into the sand.

BLOOD EAGLE

Wet, slimy trees blow sideways—

the storm is on its way.

We rationalize that our ancestors suffered

enough punishment

for the rest of us while we sit back and watch

the electric clouds gather overhead.

The gray storm air arrives and vivisects our

torsos until our lungs

burst from our backs. They gain

momentum as they flap and we fly away,

breathing and moving simultaneously.

To those who see us we are both angels and hellions,

winged and peaceful and red and bloody and sad.

You ask me why we haven't died yet.

I don't have an answer

       and that bothers you.

       We arrive at a cold mountain perch,

       our lung wings

exhausted from the distance we traveled.

When we land our lungs absorb back

into our chests.

The plan all along

was for us to end up somewhere

       impossible to leave.

       Strange, I knew this would happen

before it happened.

NOTES

Some poems are remakes of poems that other authors wrote—all of which were titled "Poem" by their respective authors (the remakes are identified with epigraphs). I twisted, bent, modified, added, and subtracted from the original source material.

All outside quotes have citations within the body of the poems.

ACKNOWLEDGMENTS

Poems in this collection have appeared in issues of the following publications, in one form or another: *<kill author, Gabby Journal, Barn Owl Review, Weave Magazine, decomP, NightBlock Magazine, Pith, Carte Blanche, Metazen,* and *Rougarou.*

I would like to thank my wife Nicole Buenaventura for being so supportive throughout my writing process. Seriously, she rocks.

A special thanks goes out to my past professors and colleagues for their help in shaping my writing, especially: Joshua McKinney, Peter Grandbois, Richard Greenfield, Carmen Giménez-Smith, Connie Voisine, Floydd Michael Elliott, and Megan Wong.

ABOUT GOLD WAKE PRESS

Gold Wake Press, an independent publisher, was founded in Boston, Massachusetts in 2008 by J. Michael Wahlgren. All in-print Gold Wake titles are available at Amazon, barnesandnoble.com, and via order from your local bookstore.

Mary Quade's *Local Extinctions*

Joshua Butts' *New to the Lost Coast*

Mary Buchinger Bodwell's *Aerialist*

Becca J. R. Lachman's *Other Acreage*

Lesley Jenike's *Holy Island*

Tasha Cotter's *Some Churches*

Nick Courtright's *Let There Be Light*

Kyle McCord's *You Are Indeed an Elk, But This is Not the Forest You Were Born to Graze*

Hannah Stephenson's *In the Kettle, the Shriek*

Kathleen Rooney's *Robinson Alone*

ABOUT THE AUTHOR

Adam Crittenden holds an MFA in poetry from New Mexico State University and serves as an editor for *Lingerpost* and *Puerto del Sol*. His work has appeared in *Bayou Magazine, Metazen, Matter Press, Whiskey Island, Barn Owl Review,* and other journals. Currently, he teaches writing in Albuquerque at Central New Mexico Community College.

You can find Adam Crittenden at adamcrittenden.com and through twitter via @AdamACrittenden.